How To Graduate From People College With Honors

Dr. Janice Grier

What People Are Saying About
How to Graduate From People College

Dr. Janice Grier's book "How to Graduate from People College" is a highly sought-after bestseller that would make a valuable addition to any personal library. Her writing style is both candid and informative, providing invaluable insight into areas where readers may be struggling in their interpersonal relationships. One key takeaway from the book is how to break free from seeking validation from others and reclaiming agency in your life. It helped me to move away from a victim mentality and toward a more empowered, victorious perspective. I would like to express my deepest gratitude to Dr. Grier for her eye-opening contribution to the world through this book and I look forward to reading more of her works. Finally, I send wishes for continued blessings, guidance, and success to Dr. Grier.

Dr. Pamela Green

How To Graduate from People College is a highly informative book with a very direct approach. While reading this book it opened me up to the realization that I was subjected to people's thoughts, opinions, stares, and reactions. However, this book gave many different approaches to overcoming the thoughts and judgements of others. I love this book because it taught me to live my life the way God has intended for me to live it, without the thoughts and pressures of others. My favorite chapter is Chapter 4, it starts off with quoting Jeremiah 1:5. Basically it says that God knew me before I was formed in my mother's womb and that HE had already approved me and set me apart from others.

Just knowing this alone allows me to know the only one I should seek approval from is God himself and not to try and please man and seek favor or approval from man. God loves me just the way I am because he is the one that created me.

Thelma Peoples

The title of this book is a game changer alone. "How to Graduate from People College". Sign me up I'm ready for class. Going on this journey with Dr. Grier was amazing. I realized that I was unintentionally living through the eyes of others. Always wanting to be sure that I lived up to the expectations of others. I used to worry a lot about what people would think and say regarding me and my actions. With the help of "How to Graduate from People College" and a closer relationship with God, I know that I was created to please and glorify God and that I am fearfully and wonderfully made. 2 Timothy 1:7 has given me courage. I am no longer fearful of what people might say, feel or think of me. I have the power to look to God (from which my help comes) with much love and a sound mind. I pray that this book will be as helpful to others as it was for me. To God be the Glory!

Tiffani Grier

How to graduate from people college is a God Send. So many of us deal with issues of rejection and bitterness from failed relationship, unmet needs, and expectations from those we hold high, and they fail us. This book should be labeled as a healing manuscript. Today I can say that I'm a Graduate of people college. No longer allowing people, places, or things to keep me held under the thumbs of oppression. I'm free praise the Lord I'm free!

Pastor Falisha Smith

How to Graduate from People College by Apostle Dr. Janice D. Grier is an easy-to-read guide on how to overcome past hurts that impair our growth, happiness, and success. It is a powerful guide on how to overcome painful events in our past and create a triumphant future. To be victorious in life, I concur with Dr. Grier's statement in the book's introduction, "we must be able to recognize and deal with the different emotions and frustrations that we carry from birth to adulthood, which causes us to become people pleasers. Shelia Lenoir

Contents

INTRODUCTION

As I begin writing the second half of this life changing book. How to graduate from people college? With honors. I realized that God has a purpose and a Plan For every aspect of our lives.

God gives us the gift of choice. But the consequences of our choices determine the quality of our lives. You will notice that quality and not quantity, regardless of how old we get, our lives must be filled with the quality of wanting to live it to the fullest, without the burdens of self-doubt, misplaced guilt, and stagnation based on what others erroneously think of us. Jesus promised us life and life more abundantly (John 10:10).

So why do we allow people to hold us hostage, to hinder our forward movement with what they think or speak about us? The truths in this book can help you to daily live life as an honor graduate from People College.

However, our challenge first is to pass the course of people approval: low self-esteem, rejection, insecurities, generational curses, stereotypes, fear, depression, and other strongholds that defines us.

The scripture states in Third John 1-2: *Beloved, I wish above all things that thou mayest prosper and be in health even as thy soul prospereth.*

Let's learn to live by God's word and stay free from people pleasing bondages.

How To Graduate From People College With Honors

Dr. Janice Grier

Chapter 1

Understanding Who You Are

Do you know who you really are?

When I received Christ in my life at the early age of 14, I still didn't realize who I really was in Christ until I started developing a close relationship with Christ. Although still dealing with issues of my past and trying to keep myself in a position for God to use me as time passed by, my closeness with God developed into something more than just a crush. I found myself falling in love with my Savior daily.

There is a difference between having a crush on someone and falling in love with someone. Pediaa.com defines crush as "a brief and intense infatuation with someone, while love is an intense feeling of deep love." Ask yourself these questions to help evaluate the closeness of your relationship with God: "Do I love God? Or Do I have a crush on God because He

> *We are called to glorify and serve God! Not people.*

is blessing me when I need Him to?" Genuinely loving God beyond having a crush on Him will bring you through the tests of life with flying colors.

Each test came my way I passed with God's help, each mistake I made and there were quite a few, I learned more about how not to repeat myself, but to do better every time I was faced with the oppositions of life. As I grew in God, my whole life became a life college of tests and exams day after day.

Reading and studying the Bible - God's word - is key to building an intimate passionate relationship with God. The charge to study God's word is up to us. Consider what II Timothy 2:15 says, *"Study to shew thyself approved unto God, a workman that needeth not to be ashamed, rightly dividing the word of truth."*

To meet the challenges of life as a child of God, We must study to meet the approval of God's plan and purpose for our lives. We must be a workman labor ready for the master, rightly dividing the word of truth.

The truth of God helps us to see ourselves inside and out when we realize who we are.

Our walk in Christ will become steadier without any doubt. The steps you are able to make will become easier when you come to the reality of who you are in Christ! We are His children who have been called to serve him.

We are called to glorify and serve God, not people, know who called you. Christ or people.

When we realize in our spirit that we were called by God, then we will know how to pray for God's people and not prey on his people. Think about it, which are you?

There are no big *I's* and little *you's* in God, only children in position to be used by the Father.

Jesus helped His disciples in the debate of who was greater when he spoke and said in Luke 22:26: *But he that is greatest among you, let him be as the younger; and he that is chief, as he that doth serve.* Being a servant doesn't sound good to your ego, but this is how it must be to be elevated in God.

We must realize nobody can lift us to that next level, but God, that's why I love what Matthew 23:12: *And whosoever shall exalt himself shall be abased, And he that shall humble himself, shall be exalted. We must understand we are servants of the King, not for the people!*

Our walk in Christ will become steady, unmovable, unshakable, and free of doubt.

The steps you are able to make will become easier when you come to the reality of who you really are in Christ. Who are you? His children have been called to serve him.

We are called to glorify and serve God! Not people. Know who called you, Christ, or people.

_____

_____

_____

_____

_____

_____

_____

_____

_____

_____

_____

_____

_____

_____

_____

_____

_____

_____

_____

_____

_____

_____

_____

_____

_____

Chapter 2

Accepting Your Inheritance

When I was 25 years old, my father left me some money in the form of an insurance policy. It was considered an inheritance, but the only way I could get it was to find the paperwork to prove that I was his oldest daughter, so I started an overly complex process of trying to get what was mine. I got upset when the insurance adjuster didn't believe the paperwork that I was sending them. I became upset at one point and decided it was not worth the trouble of having someone tell me that I was not entitled to the money that was rightfully mine.

After calming down and meditating on God's word in Psalms 24:1: *The earth is the Lord's, and the fulness thereof; the world, and they that dwell therein* I started the process of fighting for my inheritance, and I received it. I had to change my mindset from having just enough to having more than enough.

> *You can't allow anyone or anything to become a mental roadblock between you and your inheritance from God.*

Take a look at the children of Israel, their inheritance was the promised land that God had already preserved for them. But the

22

roadblocks of their past kept preventing them from possessing what belonged to them as heirs. Deuteronomy 6:3: *Hear, therefore O Israel, and observe to do it, that it may be well with thee, and that you may increase mightily, as the Lord God of my fathers has promised thee, in the land that flows with milk and honey.*"

God wants us to have our inheritance, but we have to get rid of the bondages of the past and overcome the opinions of others that weight us down.

We must deal with the old thoughts of addiction approval before we can possess our new mindset of confidence. We have to ask God to renew and change our old mindsets of settling for a life of mediocrity and accept our inheritance of being free from the bondage of stereotypes. We must rehearse His Word from Deuteronomy 28:13: *And the Lord shall make thee the head, and not the tail, and thou shall be above only, and thou shall not be beneath.*

You can't allow anyone or anything to become a mental roadblock between you and your inheritance from God.

To live full and quality lives, that is, live in our Godly inheritance, we must pass the roadblock courses in life's journey. The good news is these courses are passable and great benefits come with passing them. Prayer, praise and studying God's word are some victory tools for moving into and enjoying our inheritance. Deuteronomy 26:1 tells us, *"And it shall be, when thou art come in unto the land which the LORD thy God giveth thee*

24

for an inheritance, and possessest it, and dwellest therein;"

I accept my inheritance from my God to live a full and fruitful life without the backlash of the opinions of others. My life cannot be lived by someone else's opinion, it is by my opinion and my choices. I know who I am!

_____
_____
_____
_____
_____
_____
_____
_____
_____
_____
_____
_____
_____
_____
_____
_____
_____
_____
_____
_____
_____
_____
_____
_____
_____
_____
_____
_____

_____

_____

_____

_____

_____

_____

_____

_____

_____

_____

_____

_____

_____

_____

_____

_____

_____

_____

_____

_____

_____

_____

_____

_____

Chapter 3

Beware of the Spiritual Energy Snatchers

I'm reminded of a time ten years ago when the ministry was just beginning to flow into deeper waters of the vision that God had given me. I found myself in a spiritual drought. I was drained day in and day out because the work of the ministry was heavy.

At that time neither my friends nor my church associates could help me. Church members were pulling on my anointing, and I was feeling desolate, but no one picked up on my condition. No one had anything uplifting for me to hold on to. There was no one who gave me a word from God. As a leader I was constantly giving out, but I also needed refueling.

I decided I could not go on any longer in this condition. I knew I needed to initiate a rescue plan to pass the course of energy snatchers. The chief component of my rescue plan was simple, yet essential. I started spending quality time with God who is all powerful and not with people whom I thought had strength.

Protect your destiny. Protect your mind, by understanding who you are in God.

So, on a daily basis, I spent two hours in God's presence for five days, and God revealed to me that I have allowed the enemy to steal my energy. My zeal and joy to move forward was draining out because of negative conversations. People were not aware they were being used by the enemy to sabotage the move of God in my life and my mind.

We have to be careful because family members and friends and even church folks will drain you if you allow it to happen, They will become Satan's host, And you won't realize it until it's too late." Stated by Dr. Jacquie Hadnot, *"Don't be the devil's host."* You must protect your destiny and protect your mind by understanding who you are in God.

The Bible says the enemy comes for three things. John 10-10: *The thief comes not but to steal and to kill and to destroy.*

The thief is not concerned with who he uses to accomplish his assignment. Please stop allowing people to drain you with their leftover problems that they can't solve themselves or won't try to solve.

People will drain your strength and your dreams in one conversation. I'm reminded of Jesus in Matthew 4:1-4: When he was led up by the spirit into the wilderness to be tempted of the devil.

Then was Jesus led up of the Spirit into the wilderness to be tempted of the devil. And when he had fasted forty days and forty nights, he was afterward an hungred. And when the tempter came to him, he said, If thou be the Son of God, command that these stones be made bread. But he answered and said, It is written, Man shall not live by bread alone, but by every word that proceedeth out of the mouth of God.

Satan was using the Word of God against the Son of God. He was trying to snatch Jesus' spiritual energy. He came to Jesus after His 40 days and nights of fasting. When Jesus was very hungry, the enemy tried to drain Jesus of His trust in His Father in heaven, because Jesus knew the Word the spiritual energy snatcher, Satan couldn't get the victory.

You have to do the same when messy family and friends, or weak church folks try to drain your strength and confidence in God. Fight back with the Word of God, it is the only way we will survive while on our God ordained assignments. We must at all times keep our prayer relationship alive with the father and remember who you are. 1 Peter 2:9 says, *But you are a chosen generation, a royal priesthood, a holy nation, a peculiar people that ye should shew forth the praises of him who called you out of darkness into this marvelous light.*

This scripture assures me that I am more than what people think or say about me. I refuse to let anyone snatch my God-given right to walk in my season and in God's timing for my life. People will try to snatch your dreams and vision if you are not alert to what is happening around you. Whoever you allow to speak into your ear gates can change your destiny. Bishop Willie White, a great man of God said, *"people's opinions are like having a nose, everybody got one!"*

To sum up what you have read in this chapter: Complete your assignment without being hindered by outside opinions regarding who you are. Stay focused on the greater works. First John. 4:4: *You are of God, little children. And I have overcome them. Because greater is he that is in you, then he that is in the world.*

Today I stand as an honor graduate from People College. I took the courses of life that were at times intense and most times painful, but these courses were necessary in my curriculum for me to succeed. I passed the tests that were persistently before me. I excelled, and you can excel and graduate with honors from People College.

_____

_____

_____

_____

_____

_____

_____

_____

_____

_____

_____

_____

_____

_____

_____

_____

_____

_____

_____

_____

_____

_____

_____

_____

_____

_____

Chapter 4

Just Stay Focused!

You must stay focused because your goal is to finish on top. You must stay focused and work hard in order to accomplish honor status in this people's college of life. When you stay focused no one can tell you anything contrary to what you know you went through to get to that point of overcoming being a people pleaser.

Stay focused so that you will be on top with your dreams and ambitions to always give the best of you. This is why you must repent daily and stay transparent before God.

I've been in God's service for fifty-seven years and I still have to remain humble in His presence. I have to continue to remind myself to stay focused on the assignment God has placed before me.

It is easy to be blindsided by the enemy when you are caught up in emotions. Remember, emotions have no reasoning and when you get caught up in how you believe people should see you or act towards you that is the moment you lose sight of your goals and objects. The failure to succeed enters into

Stay focused so that you will be on top with your dreams and ambitions to always give the best of you.

your subconscious and you will try to operate with a clear mind, but you cannot because of the emotional and mental blockage of seeking the approval of people. Please don't let people speak negative things in your life and change your positive mindset.

I am filled with joy when I think about the marvelous things God is manifesting in my life to help His people come to a place to live for Christ and have a life of abundance. *I am come that they might have life, and that they might have it more abundantly* (John 10:10b).

I preached about the farmer and his donkey!

It begins with the donkey trying to get some water from a bucket that was hanging over the outdoor well. As he was trying to get to the bucket of water, he accidentally fell into the well and started to make a loud noise. The farmer heard it and came running out, only to find his donkey down in the well.

The farmer did everything he could to try and get the donkey out, but to no avail. So, he started shedding tears and told the donkey I can't get you out. I will give you a decent burial. The farmer took his wheelbarrow and start pouring dirt down in the well one barrel behind the other until he could not hear or see the donkey. As the farmer walked back into the house, he heard a noise out by the well and ran out just in time to see two ears sticking up from the dirt. The farmer got the shovel and started to take the dirt out of the well. And as he continued to shovel the dirt, the Donkey lifted up his head and made a loud noise to show him that he was still alive. The farmer was filled with joy because the donkey survived the well.

Why is this story so important?

While the farmer was trying to give the donkey a good burial with the dirt every time he poured the dirt in the well, the donkey would shake it off, pack it under his feet, and got into position for the next load. Each time the donkey would do the same with the dirt until he reached the top. The donkey used the dirt for his staircase to freedom. This story is a word of encouragement to everyone who needs to finish people college.

Sometimes you may feel as if you are being covered with negative words from several directions. I challenge you to remember the farmer's donkey. Shake it off, pack it down, and keep it moving. Shake off rejection, depression. low self-esteem, fear, pride, addictions and experiences of your past, people pleasing spirits and all the things that are holding you back in your mind and with God's help make all these things be your stair steps to victory. Keep it moving you got too much to do for God. It does not matter if hate is thrown at you, let hate become stairsteps of motivation. Let your haters become your motivators.

We must remember what Psalm 118:22 says, *The stone which the builders refused is become the head stone of the corner.* This means that there will be people who:

- Won't accept you for who God called you to be.
- Won't support your vision.
- Speak unkindly of you.
- Spend time trying to discourage you.
- Reject you because you graduated from people College.

God has made your name great right before their eyes and spread a table before you in their presence. When others reject who God says you are, you have to make a decision to discount their negative words, attitudes, and actions toward you. In other words, you must shake it off, keep it moving, and stay focused.

You have to love people, even if they don't care to be around you. Jesus spoke to us in Matthew 5:46. *'But if you love them which love you, what reward have ye?* There is no reward in loving someone that loves you. But there is a great reward when you love and pray for someone who doesn't love you at all. I am a living testimony of this painful process of life, but it was necessary for my growth in Christ in order to graduate from people college with honors. To love those who don't love us is a tremendous testimony to our growth and strength in the Lord.

When you graduate with honors from people college you become sold out to God with greater intensity and you're able to take love thy neighbor to a whole new level. Jesus said in Matthew 5:44: *But I say unto you, love your enemies. Bless them that curse you, Do good to them that hate you and pray for them which despitefully use you and persecute you.*

Move on, love them anyway and Graduate!

The saying that says misery loves company can be seen in the fact that people want you to feel inadequate because they feel inadequate. When you feel bad about yourself or situation, they often take joy in your misery.

God's Word in Second Corinthians 10:5 says, *"Casting down imaginations, and every high thing that exalteth itself against the knowledge of God, bringing into captivity every thought to the obedience of Christ."* You must bring all scattered thoughts and mindsets into the captivity of God's obedience. How? By doing what Apostle Paul told the Philippians in Philippians 2:5: *Let this mind be in you, which is also in Christ Jesus.*

Jesus was an excellent example to follow as we strive to overcome the bondage of negative words spoken over us. No matter what they called Him or how they ridiculed Him, He knew who He was, the Son of God. Even when He went to his own people, they rejected Him in Matthew 13:55-58: *Is not this the Carpenter's son? Is not his mother called Mary and his brethren James and Joses, and Simon, and Judas, and his sisters, are they not all with us? And they were brilliant in him. But Jesus said unto them, a prophet is without honor save in his own country and his own house. And He did not many mighty works there because of their unbelief.*

Jesus taught us to understand that people close to you will stereotype you in a certain manner because they have become common or familiar with you. You have nothing to prove anything to anybody, stay focused on the assignment God has for you. As my dear daughter Pastor Falisha Smith would say, *"Just bloom where God has planted you."*

For years I have been a soldier for Christ, and I had to stay focused, otherwise I would not have survived the negative words and looks from people. In God's Army you have to be alert and stay focused on the battle that is before you. *If I lose too many battles, I may lose the war."* I discovered that I'm not popular in certain circles and I'm not popular with certain people. Nevertheless, I'm encouraged to say that I'm necessary for the Kingdom of God. I am a proud graduate of people college with honors.

It's time to stop being held back because of what you think people are saying concerning you. Run and don't look back. The days are over when you try to measure up to someone else's expectations. It's time to graduate from people and their manipulative mind controlling games, and let God be in control. Now you stand as the honors graduate anointed to love and appointed to lead with no regrets.

_____

_____

_____

_____

_____

_____

_____

_____

_____

_____

_____

_____

_____

_____

_____

_____

_____

_____

_____

_____

_____

_____

_____

_____

_____

_____

_____

_____

_____

_____

_____

_____

_____

_____

_____

_____

_____

_____

_____

_____

_____

_____

_____

_____

_____

_____

_____

_____

_____

_____

_____

_____

_____

_____

_____

_____

_____

_____

_____

_____

_____

_____

_____

_____

_____

_____

_____

_____

_____

_____

_____

Graduate Prayer

Lord, I decree and declare That I will no longer be under bondage of what people say or think about me! Psalms 139-14 states: *I will praise thee; For I'm fearfully and wonderfully made: Marvelous are thy works, And that my soul knoweth right well.*

Lord, you are my shepherd, and I shall not want for anything, Because you supply all my needs I thank you for redeeming me and restoring me daily with your Grace and mercy. I won't look back. I will move forward In my Divine destiny, Because I was born

Different on purpose! Father I will live in health, wealth, and spiritual revelation daily. Thank you Lord, for

Your protection and faithfulness in Jesus name. Amen.

Scriptures to Help Pass the Exam Courses of Life

Psalms 23:1-2
The Lord is my shepherd; I shall not want. He maketh me to lie down in green pastures: he leadeth me beside the still waters.

Proverbs 3:26
For the Lord shall be thy confidence, and shall keep thy foot from being taken.

1 John 5:4
For whatsoever is born of God overcometh the world: and this is the victory that overcometh the world, even our faith.

Hebrews 13:6
So that we may boldly say, The Lord is my helper, and I will not fear what man shall do unto me.

II Timothy 1:7

For God hath not given us the spirit of fear; but of power, and of love, and of a sound mind.

Isaiah 41:10

Fear thou not; for I am with thee: be not dismayed; for I am thy God: I will strengthen thee; yea, I will help thee; yea, I will uphold thee with the right hand of my righteousness.

Romans 10:7

Or, Who shall descend into the deep? (that is, to bring up Christ again from the dead.)

Deut. 28:12-13

The Lord shall open unto thee his good treasure, the heaven to give the rain unto thy land in his season, and to bless all the work of thine hand: and thou shalt lend unto many nations, and thou shalt not borrow. And the Lord shall make thee the head, and not the tail; and thou shalt be above only, and thou shalt not be beneath; if that thou hearken unto the commandments of the Lord thy God, which I command thee this day, to observe and to do them:

About the Author

Chief Apostle Dr. Janice D. Grier received Christ into her life at the age of 14. She graduated from Newton County High School with honors. She then attended Georgia State University, completing her degree in 1975. She continued to pursue her education at Dayspring Theological Seminary in Panama City, Florida and graduated in 2002.

Apostle Grier is spiritually motivated to work in the Kingdom. In 2007, she formed Reach Beyond the Break Outreach Ministries, a community outreach program that assists with food, clothing, housing, and utility assistance. God shifted the name of the ministry in 2009 from The Fellowship Church of Praise Atlanta to the New & Living Way International Deliverance Ministries, Inc.

In 2010, after serving in God's Kingdom for 44 years, God elevated Pastor Grier to the office of Apostle. In 2010, Apostle Grier started the J. Grier Christian Academy in Tucker, Georgia; it is licensed and incorporated by the state of Georgia. The J. Grier Christian Academy is now J Grier Child Development Center, which is open during spring and summer breaks, offering summer educational services for youth. In May 2011, Apostle Grier made her presence known on the air waves on Channel 57 T.V., Comcast Channel 2. Apostle Grier's first book;

"How to Graduate from People College" debuted January 2015. This must-have book is available on Amazon.

Apostle Janice Grier has received many awards, including the 2015 "Kingdom Woman of the Year" award from A Woman of Worth Empowerment Ministries, Kansas City, Missouri. In 2016 she received the "A Woman of Worth" award from Deborah's Daughter, Inc. She was recently awarded the 2018-2019 "Kingdom Educators INSPIRE" award from the New and Living Way Youth and Community Outreach Department.

In 2019, Apostle Grier returned to academic study at The School of the Great Commission Bible College and Seminary and earned her Doctor of Theology degree. In 2020 Dr. Grier was certified as a licensed Christian Counselor from the National Association of Christian Counselors. She is the Dean of the Greater New and Living Way School of the Great Commission Bible School and Seminary in Tucker, Georgia.

Additionally, Dr. Grier is the CEO of the J. Grier Community Development Center in Tucker, GA.

Made in the USA
Columbia, SC
26 May 2024

35769689R00037